THE QUARRY

Daniel Huws was born in London in 1932, his mother English, his father Welsh. For over thirty years he worked in the Department of Manuscripts of the National Library of Wales. He writes about manuscripts and traditional music, in English and Welsh.

D1157260

THE QUARRY

DANIEL HUWS

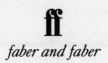

faber and faber

First published in 1999
by Faber and Faber Limited
3 Queen Square London WC1N 3AU

Photoset by Wilmaset Ltd, Wirral
Printed in England by MPG Books Limited, Victoria Square, Bodmin, Cornwall

All rights reserved

© Daniel Huws, 1999

Daniel Huws is hereby identified as author of this
work in accordance with Section 77 of the Copyright,
Designs and Patents Act 1988

'The guardians' was published as a pamphlet by the Sceptre Press
(under the title *Buzzards*) in 1974, 'From an old songbook' in
PN Review no. 1, and 'Three its' in *Poetry Wales*.
The poems in Part Two are taken from *Noth* (Secker & Warburg, 1972);
Part Three, 'Al poco giorno', was published in *Chequer* in 1954.

*This book is sold subject to the condition that it shall not,
by way of trade or otherwise, be lent, resold, hired out or
otherwise circulated without the publisher's prior consent in
any form of binding or cover other than that in which it is
published and without a similar condition including this
condition being imposed on the subsequent purchaser*

A CIP record for this book
is available from the British Library

ISBN 0-571-19711-6

2 4 6 8 10 9 7 5 3 1

CONTENTS

PART ONE

FROM AN OLD SONGBOOK

The girl was sensational, he was a creep,
His eyes were like pebbles while hers were so deep
That at night the thought of them left me no sleep
They so plainly knew something was lacking.

As I leaned on this tree I could only advise
That touch it or eat it sure nobody dies
Of a bite of the fruit that will open your eyes
Till like gods you gaze out on the garden.

But somehow we managed to cock up the show
By upsetting the gaffer, old who-do-you-know,
Your one with the voice who's accustomed to go
For his walk in the cool of the evening.

And she whom I love goes eating her bread
In the sweat of a bloke who'd be happier dead
While the horny heels come bruising my head
As I choke on the dust of the desert.

So you beasts of the field take warning by me
However so subtle you think you may be
Keep your tongues to yourselves or the Old Man will see
That you drag out your days on your bellies.

THE GUARDIANS

Lift your eyes to heaven
And you suddenly see them,
Two guardian angels,
High above the valley,
Moving apart,
Moving together,
Looping
On invisible swell.

It isn't a love dance,
It isn't a duel,
They are feeding their young.

They nest high
In the tall oak
In the shrunken core
Of the old wood.

There is no other pair for miles.

THE PRIEST'S CONFESSION

Father, I'm troubled by Satan, afraid I begin
To discover his works in places where
My theology hadn't conceived them,
In coloured cloth and in agitation of air.

The enormity dawned when I met the widow's daughter
(A woman by now, I have to confess)
And found myself exclaiming
Well, glory be, my child, what a lovely dress.

And meant it but suddenly thought can the glory of God
Reside in a beautiful dress on a girl.
Is it not of the Devil's making?
Think of music and think of a dress awhirl.

Last night my cousin came home from sea and we all
Went down to Matt's for a couple of jars,
And a stranger fiddler was playing
And I walked home late and unsteady under the stars.

So standing alone at the altar this morning, Father,
With the body of Christ in my hands I said
The words without thought of their meaning
And last night's new reel ran round and round in my head.

THE PRINT

They have taken the body away
But have left him here.
Day-old tobacco smoke
Meets you at the door
Of the unwarmed house.

Food waits on the table,
A last shopping,
And fumbled lists.
A vest is hanging to dry.
With what ingenuity
The old survive.
Here in stains and dust
Is the print of how it is done.

By water and fire
A weeping detective
Destroys the evidence.

GOODBYE

He had driven them far away, wife and children,
Without knowing how. Surely they would return?
And now the *Radio Times* came round so fast,
There were tumbling walls to rebuild and trees to plant,
So much to plan in the house that had been his past.

His litany of defeat you tried to stem
With words and words until time came to go.
How easy that Sunday night to disregard
Why in that bare kitchen, although you promised
To be back within the month, he hugged so hard.

THE QUARRY

The quietness,
They have all scattered
Into the maze of gorse
And slabs of rock,
In tattered jerseys
And faded frocks.

Ages ago,
And I still stand
Caught in the long afternoon
In the old quarry,
Face to the wall,
Counting to twenty.

NEW MOON

The sun is down and the ridge-line
Of trees moves into focus.

Your fields stiffen with frost.
Forget the walk to the hilltop
And the sight of that new moon slipping
Into the sea. Turn home.

Wrapped in their breath
Your cattle stamp at the gate.

INDELICATE

Served by the quiet woman with the brown eyes
In the delicatessen indelicate even to think
That the sound when she turns aside and movingly
Slices salami evokes the jingle of bedsprings.

THREE ITS

It wasn't much,
It wouldn't last long,
A crust and a bottle of water,
And how he was dying to share it.

It was that sort of place,
A kind of Sahara.
If you met someone in the middle of it
You wouldn't call it chance.

The sun lifts into the sky again
To a chorus of bread and water.

PALAIS D'AMOUR

The cabaret comes to climax
At the lit end of a crowded hall
As a mumbling transvestite thrusts
A cup in the air in triumph.

In shadow beside a disturbed
Ocean of heads a watchful madame
In her own space, to her own music,
Dances her baby to sleep.

AS WHEN

As when in a city
Where once you felt at home
You take your place in the café,
And coffee steams, cigar-smoke
Drifts across and voices
Dissolve to liturgy,

As when, faint with walking,
You enter a church,
Sit at the end of a pew
Alone in a great vault
And listen for silence,

As when you slip into a bar
With its glass and mahogany,
Put down your drink,
Settle yourself in a corner
And close your eyes,

Time wavers,
Time falls away.

If a passing angel
Proposed you build an altar
You would no more demur

Than you would to raise a cairn,
Above the forest,
Above the cloud,
In the shiver of dawn on a peak.

A CADENCE

In tremulous script he wished a Happy Christmas
And Bright New Year to the widow of his friend
On the flyleaf of *British Flora*, and there he added:
My mother and I used this when we went for walks
Beyond Queen's Road when I was a little boy
Between 1884 and 89
And in those days we found many wild flowers
In the summer by the banks of the Mersey.

THE SLOW WAY

The slow way home was through the wood
Which creaked with age

And down the steep slope
Which gorse was rewinning

And, as light failed,
Along the green lane where water streamed

And in the November storm
The red campion battled so late.

MORE THAN GLASS

Speeding by train to a city
To a sad cremation,
Cut off by more than glass
From the bloomed hayfields,
From the child with satchel standing
In morning sun at the end of a lane.

PEACE

How come you find peace
In the heart of a city
With three old women
And one young man

In a fusty cavity
Where the hopes of uncounted prayers
And nuptials and requiems
Spiral and hang

Like cigarette smoke
At the height of a party
Eternally.

SILENCE

Dead?

From a window?

Was she very depressed?

The receiver reposes.

The drop of silence
Becomes a lake.

FIRST NIGHT

Open-eyed in bed,
Effigies on a tomb.
Outside is starry and bright-rimmed
Clouds are traversing the window
Making their quick condolence.

Deep in a new first night,
Past all but holding hands,
Not a word, not a stir, nor now
Any sobs any more.

HILLFORT

This hazy unwonted
Dry October draught
From the hills to the east
Has blanched the fields,
Has crusted the mud in the gateways.

Has impaled on the gorse
Of the scarry ramparts
A shivering array
Of votive bronze and gold
From the hangings below.

Poised on the rim,
The ancient ones,
The thorn with its haws
And oak with the last
Of its leaves bow into the wind.

THE ORNITHOLOGIST'S FRIEND

The ornithologist, like a doctor
Pronouncing my dissolution, said they were gone.
Lapwings which years ago had abandoned the lowlands
Could no longer be found in the hills, not in these parts.

But he was wrong, for two peewits cry
As they stumble and slide in air like men in snowdrifts
Above the field by the mountain road where I walked
With a headful of sounds which came from no creature on
    earth.

No, my darlings, I've too many secrets already.
What would I give to know that you had kept yours,
To find you in twelve months' time drunkenly wheeling,
Summoning me away from your airy domain
Where the gelding stands alone in the field full of rushes.

AT THE ROOT OF BEING

FROM THE WELSH OF WALDO WILLIAMS

At the root of being there is no decay,
The heartwood survives.
Courage there is the tenderness
Of the life of all frail lives.

That is where after the storm the heart withdraws.
The world's not right,
But in this low redoubt the squirrel of happiness
Makes its nest tonight.

MERCY

Ritual, said the Sister of Mercy,
What words can not express.
She was speaking of bereavement.

Mourners stepped off the boat.
A couple sat on a casing,
Unmoving, no longer young.

What dangers had he survived?
What affection could he have deserved
As he gazed out to sea

While she cushioned her head
On the shoulder of his jacket
And fingered his buttons like a baby?

THE EDGE OF A PLAYGROUND

As disenchantement,
A drawing away
From family,
From attentive loved ones,

Steals, you imagine,
Like dawning light
Regardlessly
To the slowly dying,

So disenchantment
Can strike like lightning
In the calm of a day
With nearest long-not-seen-ones,

And strike for instance
At the edge of a playground
Crowded with children.
So little is called for.

Simply two strangers
On a neighbouring seat
Half-watching a child,
Simply a shock of red hair,
A face and a laugh.

THE ROCK

Sea campion in the pocket,
Thrift in the cleft of the rock.
Below, garlands of seaweed,
A tract of sand washed clean
And waves retreating.

Beyond the grey, beyond the green, the blue,
And beyond the blue,
The parting we call the horizon.

A WINTER CALENDAR

A garden expectant,
Hedge-shadows black,
Moonlight shining
From dew on the cabbage leaves.

※

The chestnut stark
In the pale meadow,
Her dress a circle
Of gold on the floor at her feet.

※

Stones hoary,
Molehills like rock,
The thistles withdrawn
To their frosty crystalline core.

※

A frozen stream,
Mouthings,
Words trying to form,
Bubbles under the ice.

※

Clouds build,
The moon goes under,
Sleepless companions
Hear the rain arrive.

※

A last tattoo
And the squall is past,
Gutters quaver,
A blackbird begins to sing.

WOODSMOKE

We followed the footpath through the wood.
There was the house,
Its ivy-gripped stone,
Its primrosy garden stepped to a river
Loud in a rock-strung bed.

The gamekeeper we had reckoned on meeting
Was on his rounds.
But his young wife
Had us sit down and we talked of spring
And the shelteredness of the place.

You're the first to have called all winter, she laughed
As we said goodbye.
And my hand lingered
In the hand of the child on the arm of the woman
Of the house that was drenched in woodsmoke.

PART TWO

THE PARTY

'All I meet is Tom, Dick and Harry
Where I hoped for a girl who would change it all.
To make this a party not a funeral
A good deal of drink seems necessary.'

So he drank and his drollery made them all laugh
Till they cried. They thought him the wonder of men.
But the crowd did not grow on his fancy and when
The room began swimming he thought he'd be off.

They pleaded with him, they gently urged
'The party's not yet over, come,
Just one more drink.' But right away home
On twelve staggering legs he lurched.

The front door slammed like a thunder of stones.
So sound they slept, not a neighbour stirred.
The air was close and he was tired.
He took off his flesh and lay in his bones.

ESCAPE

To have woken into the clear of evening
With the tired feet wandering as they please
Across the avenues of an orchard
Where green cherries are thick on the trees,

And beyond the lane where the barbarous scent
Of mayflower billowed as did its white foam
In the short hour that is not yet night
To have strayed in a wood which seemed like home,

Where birch was birch and oak true oak
And their leaves spread a darkening green.
So much was certain. But the ringing song
Was of birds more nameless than they ever have been.

WAKING IN THE SMALL HOURS

Suppose you had slept in a room for half a year
And never known that the little patch of sky
Visible from your bed, no larger than a pane,
Lay in the path of the moon.

You awake in the small hours and a foot away
On the colourless pillow two pinhead-sized full moons
Are reflected in the grey eyes staring past you
From a luminous white face.

Can wives be allowed such night-time liberties?
To startle honest husbands out of their wits,
To wander centuries away, to bind themselves
To the moon, with the gaze of a corpse?

EVEN SO

You were so beautiful, he so unwise
To protract an exchange that led to nothing.
If you'd studied his hands instead of his eyes
You might have guessed why, and even so
He'd have earned your shrug when you got up to go.

NOTHING

You appear again, more beautiful than ever,
And still he makes no move. Is he unmanned?
Nothing can spell the terrible word never
When it's made of gold. Look at his left hand.

A MOUNTAIN LAND

Broad-plained neighbours suspiciously circle
Our land of mountain; to whose small eyes
Our smiling self-sufficiency
Must speak riches.
                    One then another,
Time and again they mass their borders,
Prepared for resistance we never offer.
The sortie here, the thrust there,
Whole armies trampling our countryside,
We give like air, take to the hills.
They never stay.
                    Nothing to plunder,
No one to conquer, their mettle rusts.
They leave, arrogant and disdainful
Of the empty land that rigged their hope.
And glad always to see their backs,
To know our immunity proved again,
We laugh at their crudeness and bafflement.

But our malcontents have a fine scorn
And a harsh name for the ancient wisdom
That keeps us free. They resent that fools
Should think us beggars, feel shame we never
Have shown the nerve to commit our lives
To the flat valleys, let a nation root
And bloom a flower of civilization,
The being our richer selves a trophy
Continually to be battled for
In bloodshed in the mouths of valleys.

O MOUNTAIN

We know our crags, our climbs, our controlled terrors,
As we know our own hearthsides. We manage nicely.

The clouds of selfishness rift and terribly
Turning our foothills small and grubby appears
The mountain soaring against a blue heaven,
Bulking beyond conceivable ascent.
Yet while we slept was a breaking body climbing.

Where the winds of the world pour unendingly
Wildly whistling to no one, let the mind hover
And its eye make out in the dazzle, O Mountain, O Man,
The frail figure on the white virgin peak.

GIVE ME A MEDAL

The voice that had breathed down their necks,
        on whose strings they had danced,
Floated away beyond the trees,
Left them presenting arms on the parched square,
An infinite blankness the point of their stare.

A mate is gibbering, a mate is out cold,
Will our hero not break ranks, stir to their aid?
He doesn't bat an eye. God, give him a medal,
Your most beautiful fucking soldier on parade.

GOODBYE TO TUDOR

In forgiving mood, this sultry July afternoon,
The last lingering child will be gone
From the gates of Tudor Secondary Modern School,
A school most teachers gratefully shun.

The intimate daily struggle so calmly ends,
Without victory to either side.
Goodbye to the staff and to the boys more sadly
And the girls most sadly I have replied.

And a friend offers congratulations, echoing
Complaints I should have kept unsaid:
'My God, you must be glad to leave.' My children,
For his ignorance I could strike him dead.

THE HOUSE OF SELF-DESTRUCTION

Ominously did the planets foregather
In the twelfth house so full of danger
To the crab in his massive shell who would rather
Sidle a mile than meet a stranger.

REVENANT

A boatman used to ferry me back down the river
To the watergate. Twelve slippery stone steps
And I'd fifty yards to go along the cobbles
Past skinny kids like maggots in the dust
And beggars asleep in the shade. Then, how cool
To enter the marbled hall, how composing
To climb the grand stair, how rich with silence
My noble rooms. Not a soul dared cross my sight.

The water laps the same massive foundations.
The ground-floor windows are grated still. But above
Are windows flung wide open and washing hung out,
Shrill tongues and a woman's raucous singing.
Proliferous humankind has come to stay.

Between the walls defaced, up the littered stairs,
I fight a way in the ebb and flow of children.
I am unknown. My friends are a dead species.
My servants are swallowed up in their own lives.
My beautiful courtesans will be prinking themselves
For boys on scooters.

                What might marriage have saved?

I climb to the nursemaid's garret. The door's ajar,
The room empty. Here it is almost quiet.
The sunshine is creeping inward over the tiles.
I tiptoe across to the open casement and shiver
In the sudden warmth. There are fishermen out on a raft.
The child again, I cringe from the sheer drop
To where the diminutive ripples coruscate.

IS THE SNOW YOUR WHOLE LOVE?

For long hours the toys have lain neglected.
A face settles to glumness at the window.
Onto the paths and grass, onto the hedges,
Onto the fields and wood the flakes feather,
Down, down, to instant evanescence.
Must it be a winter without snow?

Child, child, is the snow your whole love?
Is a winter your whole lifetime?
The sky may exhaust itself in vain. Learn
To accommodate your adversary, the earth.
Snow is accidental to her gestations.
Her moods are yours for the taking, but not to be mended.

THE BURDEN

A rush of disregard, a protruding stone,
A moment of sick-faint at the crack of glass:
No other demijohn in the world can help you,
Watching the wine pulsing into the ground.

FOR BETTER FOR WORSE

The children are all asleep.
They have filled my day
As in a few years
Their absence will.
The homeland in which no longer
Should I feel at home
Is beyond the sea.
A room away my husband broods
On himself only
If he hasn't gone to bed.

There is all this heap of mending.

I am so lonely.

LIKE A STONE

When not asleep I could hear the air's faint humming,
The unmown grass was cool to the limbs, the sun
Was a glow beyond the walls of the eye's red womb.

I heard your approach, a light swishing of grass.
Blue-grey was the glaring world to my opened eyes,
And there was your outstretched arm, unwavering, pale,
Holding the russet fruit
So sternly towards me, with not a word, and your eyes
As I'd never seen them before. My will was yours.

In gratuitousness your action wanted nothing.
Can a man not be left to drowse in the sun on his own?
That was a place where I could have lain for ever,
Like a cat, like a lizard, like a stone.

NURSERY RHYME

We found the table bare
And bare the larder shelves.
We slipped to an upper room
And helped ourselves to ourselves.

WEDLOCK'S SUMMER

A billion blades of grass,
A hundred sodden roses,
Four swallows finding their wings,
Two asses rubbing noses.

THE CALL OF THE RING

He wasn't Napoleon or Byron or God.
He disapproved of trying to seem odd.
He'd cashed his life to skip and spar
And tonight he'd be greater than Tommy Farr.

There is no one to tell him it isn't his guts,
His feints, his footwork and uppercuts
That amaze the crowd that has stopped to stare
At a naked man fighting the air.

THE OFFICE

He was always the quiet sort,
Can't say I've really known him
Though I've been here as long as he has,
Thirty-three odd years.
Given his cushy old job,
A nice little wife, as they say,
And decent kids, Christ
Knows what bug can have bitten him.

Well there he was at his desk,
Arms sort of pinioned to his chair
And body sort of thrust forward,
Staring out of the window
With this god-awful look on his face,

And as if we simply weren't there
In his deadly monotone
The poor old bugger was going on
About somebody called Elias.

RENDEZVOUS

Perhaps best not tomorrow
But thirty years tomorrow,
And find how the essences mingle
After time's distillation.

Thirty expectant years,
What a vigil for us to savour.
And how poignant will be our condolence
For the flight of what might have been.

How decidedly more adult,
How far more imaginative
Than to meet precariously now
Alive to what could be.

FOUR APPROPRIATIONS

Slow major rode ahead,
Slow captain stumbled after
To tell him all the squaddies were dead
Of an unidentified laughter.

~

His milk was untouched, the police were told,
His soup was congealed and his corpse was cold
And under his shirt they found a locket
Containing nothing and made of gold,
Containing nothing, not even, not even,
Not even a woman's hair.

~

He was ambling up through the field and moved in
For his run on the rails when what do you know
He got caught in a pocket till past the post
With a handful of horse and nowhere to go.

~

A length of linen of deadest white
Waiting for the morning light
And an old woman of failing sight
And thick of nail to sew me tight.

IN THE CAFÉ

Yes, he kept saying,
Ours was a beautiful revolution,
But we should have seen his.
Her eyes, he said,
I can't tell you.
He pulled out this old photograph.

    A photograph of a wide square
    Dotted with the small figures
    Of unmistakably grown-up men
    Caught in apparently private performance
    Of the several acts of stumbling
    And running and lying prone.

A sort of memento, he explained,
The only one.
She would never give me her portrait.
Yes, it was certainly love,
Calf-love maybe,
All I have known.

    His mind was going.

FEELERS

The war goes dead.
The dead go uncounted.
New missiles are trained.
The General Staff
Is immured in conclave,
Teeth and tongue
Hatching new horror
In a blacked-out mouth.

They will not have been told
Of the peace feelers
Already out,
The hands and fingers
About their business
As they know how,
Gauche as Christ,
Adroit as the devil.

CRIME PASSIONNEL

Curtain up, says the night sky.
Enter, two blokes.
Off, a bird's disconsolate noises.

And here they come once more, says the street,
Do they think I lead nowhere?
Am I a closed circuit?

The telephone cased in its kiosk
Hums and sighs.

The letter-box gapes.

No, I can't bear it,
Says the house-door, getting hysterical.
They're here again,
And this time they're coming indoors.
One of them's a maniac, can't you see,
And lethally armed.

Exactly, says the night sky,
And as for that female party
Waiting for lover-boy,
If she can't cry herself to sleep
She's got a long night coming.

But the single bed is a bed of the world
And croaks:
I won't say I care for corpses
No more than I care for murderers
But the two of you need some kip.
I'm easy.
Make yourselves welcome.

A VOICE

Mindlessly,
Year after year,
In the same month,
In the same spot,
In the same colours,
The orchids flower,
The orchids wither.

This is the wilderness
Where a voice is crying
For the helmeted men to roll up
With their yellow plant.

THE VILLETTA

Here is your villetta
With its view over the sea
Owned by the crooked lawyer.

Here is the shack
Of the fisherman
Ready to hire out his daughter.

Here is the office
Of the head of police
Who can fix a permit of sojourn

And might not be blind
To a gift
If the gift is made
In mortification,
The coin of the realm.

ALPINES

The village in love
With the avalanche
Preens itself in the sun.

The lake in love
With the meteor
Licks its lips.

The glacier in love
With the next valley
Inches towards the sea.

A DAWN

There was no sunrise,
Only a brightening,
And the mist
Moving among the stones
Grew visible.
And there was silence,
A silence growing
Around the unanswered voices
Adrift in the chasm below,

The lament of sheep,
The call of crow,
The shuffle of shale down the scree.

ON THE MOUNTAIN

Flowers, flowers, flowers,
The mountain is moidering.

From beyond what ages of ice
Might a memory have carried?

Where have they known flowers,
These acres of rock and peat
Their cryptogams inhabit?

PLAYING WITH FIRE

Did your bonfire stream
To heaven in sparks
Or smoulder and sweat
And never flare?

I no more know
Than you can smell
The smoke in your hair.

EYES

These wide-awake eyes
And starry skies
And eyes and eyes
And wrinkles and lashes
And cheeks and lips
And hands and hands
And thighs and thighs.

And there is this lidless eye
Raking the earth
And raking the sky
For darkness.

THE PIERCING WIND

Was there not wood to hew
And stone to quarry?
Had you not eyes?
Had you not hands?

The piercing wind questions.

Answerless,
I huddle behind children.

PART THREE

AL POCO GIORNO

AFTER DANTE

Alas! we have come to the long sweeping shadow
And the short day, to the whitening of the hills
As the summer colour fades from the grass.
And still my tender longing remains green
As ever, though rooted on the cruel stone
Which speaks and hears as though it were a lady.

So alas this extraordinary lady
Stands frigid, as the snow within the shadow;
For she is not moved any more than stone
By the spring sunshine that warms the hills,
Turning them once more from white to green,
Covering them with flowers and with grass.

When she appears, her head wreathed in grass,
Displaced are thoughts of any other lady;
So beautifully formed about the green,
The golden waves lure love into their shadow,
Love who has bound me between the little hills
A thousand times more firmly than cemented stone.

Her beauty is more pure than precious stone;
Her wounds will not be soothed by healing grass;
I have struggled over plains and hills
Trying to escape this fatal lady;
And from her light no wall afforded shadow,
Neither did sheer mountain, nor forest's green.

I have seen her so lovely, dressed in green,
That she would have planted in the hardest stone
The love that I accord her very shadow;
So I have wooed her in a soft field of grass,
Fragrant and tempting as any lady,
And sheltered low among the highest hills.

Indeed, the streams will flow back to the hills
Before this young sapling, fresh and green,
Catch fire from me (as should a loving lady),
From me who would endure to sleep in stone
My whole life, and pasture in fields of grass,
Could I but gaze where glides her mantle's shadow.

Where there falls from the hills the blackest shadow,
Beneath a brilliant green this gracious lady
Drowns it, as one buries a stone in the grass.